THE BOOK OF
DANIEL
STUDY HELPS

By
Kurt Kennedy, M(BS), D.Min.

ACKNOWLEDGEMENTS

I would like to offer much thanks to John Knowles for the countless hours he spent proofreading this pamphlet, to my wife Wendy for the layout and graphic design, and to my Institute students for following me through this study of Daniel.

PREFACE

Why is the Book of Daniel so important? Why is this book of prophecy commented on by both religious and non-religious persons alike, more than any other? I believe it is because in this book God reveals when His Theocratic Kingdom will be established on the earth. It is Daniel that gives us the time factor needed for all other prophetic scriptures. Without the book of Daniel you have no order with which to place all the prophetic events found throughout scripture. Daniel is the key to unlocking the "when" of prophetic events. When does the tribulation period transpire, when is the abomination setup in the holy place, when does the antichrist come against Israel and when does God establish His long awaited Theocratic Kingdom on the earth, yes Daniel answers the when. And while we may not be able to agree on all the nuances contained in this great book, we can all agree on the overall time factor laid out before us in Daniel; the time when the God of heaven will establish His Kingdom on this earth.

"When ye therefore shall see the abomination of desolation, spoken of by Daniel the prophet, stand in the holy place, (whoso readeth, let him understand:) (Matthew 24:15)

INTRODUCTION

Historical Captivities:

Northern Tribes: Assyria took the 10 northern tribes of Israel into captivity under King Shalmaneser (2 *Kings 17:1-6, 23*). Fourteen years later Senacherib, King of Assyria, came against Judah and took the fenced cities (*2 Kings 18:13*). King Senacharib desired to take Jerusalem as well, but God miraculously delivered it (*2 Kings 19:32-35*).

Southern Tribes: Even though God had miraculously delivered Jerusalem from the Assyrian King Senacherib, He would later allow the Babylonians to come and take it. The reasons for God allowing the captivity of Judah are as follows:

1. Hezekiah, king of Judah, allowed the heathen kings from Babylon to see all treasures of the House of the Lord (*2 Kings 20:12-21*)

2. Judah worshiped heathen gods, turning from the one true God, just as the northern tribes had done previously (*Israel: 2 Kings 17:7-18! Cf. Judah: 2 kings 21:10-16*)

3. With the people in captivity, the land could enjoy its Sabbaths, which they did not keep. (*2 Chronicles 36:21*).

Destruction of Jerusalem: The destruction of Jerusalem took place in three sieges: The First siege was in approximately 606 B.C. during the reign of Jehoiakim. During this time Daniel and others were taken to Babylon (*2 Kings 24:1,2, 10; Daniel 1:1*). The Second siege was during the reign of Jehoiachin, in approximately 598 B.C. Nebuchadnezzer again came against Jerusalem, and others were taken (2 *Kings 24:11-17*). Zedekiah was then made king in Jerusalem by Nebuchadnezzar. The Third and final siege was in approximately 586 B.C. when Zedekiah rebelled against the king of Babylon, and his deputy came against Jerusalem (2 *Kings 25:1-21*).

Nebuchadnezzar and the First Revelation: Israel now finds herself scattered among the nations and surrounded by foreign tongues, which God foretold through the prophets (*Jeremiah 5:15*). Through the prophets He also said He would speak to them through these unknown tongues (*Isaiah 28:11, 33:19*). However our Lord will restore their pure language one day (*Zeph. 3:9*).

Placement of the Book of Daniel: Daniel is almost in the middle of all the prophets. God's intent is that all the information provided in the books of the prophets be placed on the prophetic timeline now revealed through Daniel.

Writing of the Book of Daniel: It is also notable that the book of Daniel was originally written in two languages. *Hebrew* is used in Daniel 1:1 - 2:4a and 8:1 - 12:13, while Aramaic (*or Chaldean*) is found in 2:4b - 7:28. This is due to the fact that the revelations concern the Gentile world powers as they rule over Israel with chapter nine dealing with God's hope for the Jewish people in the coming of the Savior.

Daniel Himself: Daniel was most probably only a young man when he was taken into captivity. Daniel lives through the entire Babylonian captivity, 70 years. Internal evidence points to Daniel being the writer (*8:1; 9:2,20; 10:2*). Externally, the Lord spoke of this book as written by Daniel (*Matt. 24:15; Mark 13:14*).

Theologically: The book itself focuses on the sovereignty of God in completing His plan and purpose in the earth. He will establish His kingdom over all other kingdoms of this world. The book of Daniel gives us the time schedule from the captivity to the Kingdom of Heaven being established on the earth. This book gives us the outline into which all other prophetic passages are to be placed.

CHAPTER ONE

The Captivity (vs. 1): In the third year of the reign of Jehoiakim king of Judah (605 BC) the *First Siege* against Judah takes place. This will mark the beginning of the *Times of the Gentiles* (Luke 21:24-28). It will be at the end of these Gentile rulers that the God of heaven will come and deliver Israel and set up His theocratic kingdom (Daniel 2:35, 44). * *Two indicators- Daniel 2:44, "kingdom of God/ kingdom of Heaven."*

The Lord Gave (vs. 2): It was the Lord that allowed the Babylonians to take Jerusalem. The Lord had made a covenant with Israel. They would be His chosen people, and as they walked in the paths of God, they would be the light to the Gentiles (Gen.12; Isa. 42:6); but if they failed to obey God and walked in the paths of the heathen Gentiles, God would chasten them and scatter them among the Gentiles (Lev. 26: 27-34).

Vessels Taken (vs. 2): The Babylonians took "part" of the "vessels" of the house of God into the land of Shinar (Babylon); king Belshazzar would later use these "vessels" to praise the heathen gods (Dan. 5:1-4). Shinar is Babylon and is most infamous in scripture (Gen. 11:1-9, Rev. 18).

School of Learning (vss. 3-7): Daniel and his three friends *(Hananiah, Mishael and Azariah)* were taken and put into language school for three years so they might stand before the king (1:5). The goal of the Babylonians was to transform them from Jews to Babylonians. Notice that *"God gave"* the four Hebrew children knowledge and skill in all learning and wisdom, and Daniel had understanding in all visions and dreams.

Trial in School (vss. 8-16): Daniel asked to not defile

himself with the portion of the king's meat nor with the wine (8). The defilement would be things offered to idols and if the meat was not drained of blood, etc. As God was the one who gave them their learning so "God had brought Daniel into favour and tender love with the prince of the eunuchs" (9). Melzar agreed to "prove" them 10 days with only water and pulse *(beans, lentils)* (12-14). They pass the test, as is described in verse 15.

Ten Times Better (vss. 17-20): Daniel and his three friends are found 10 times better than all that were in the realm among the Chaldeans (20).

Daniel's Long Life (vs. 20): Daniel was in captivity in Babylon from 605 B.C. to King Cyrus (539 B.C.), even to the 3rd year of King Cyrus (537 B.C.). He would witness the rule of Nebuchadnezzar, Darius, Belshazzar and Cyrus.

CHAPTER TWO

The King's Dream (vs. 1): The king dreamed a dream that he did not remember (8) apart from the fact that his spirit troubled him, and his sleep break from him (1).

The Challenge (vss. 2-6): The king called forth all the wise men of Babylon to give him not only the <u>interpretation</u> but also make known unto him the <u>dream</u> itself (3-5). If the wise men are able to do this they will receive a reward (6) but if not they will be cut in pieces and their houses made a dunghill (5).

The Wise Men's Response (vss. 7-11): The wise men assure the king that there is none upon the earth that can show him the matter (10), for it is a rare thing he asks. Only the gods whose dwelling is not with flesh can show the king his dream (11).

The Command (vss. 12-13): The king therefore commands all the wise men of Babylon to be slain; this would include Daniel and his three friends (13).

Daniel's Response (vss. 14-23): Daniel finds out from Arioch, the captain of the king's guard, why the king has ordered to destroy the wise men of Babylon (14-15). Then Daniel goes in to the king and asks for time to give the king the interpretation (16). Daniel and his three friends ask for mercy from God to know the interpretation, that they might not be destroyed (17-18). Daniel receives the interpretation and blesses the God of Heaven (19-23).

Daniel Before the King (vss. 24-30): Daniel assures the king that the interpretation is not by his own power, or by his three years of training by Nebuchadnezzar, but rather the "God in Heaven that revealeth secrets" (28). The dream is concerning what shall be hereafter"

(28,29).

The Vision (vss. 31-35): The vision is of a "great image" whose form was "terrible" (31). A synopsis of the image is in verses 32 & 33 and is as follows:

- Head of Gold
- Breast and arms of Silver
- Belly and thighs of Brass
- Legs of Iron
- Feet part Iron and part Clay

Then Daniel sees a stone, cut out without hands, smite the image in the feet and break them to pieces (34) until they are as chaff that the wind drives away (35), and the stone cut out without hands becomes a great mountain and fills the whole earth (35).

The Interpretation (vss. 36-45): Gentile kingdoms that make up the "times of the Gentiles" will rule over Israel until the God of Heaven sets up His kingdom.

- Head of Gold (37-38)= *Nebuchadnezzar's kingdom*
- Breast and arms of Silver (32,39 8:20)= *Medo-Persian Empire*
- Belly and thighs of Brass (39, 8:21)= *Greece*
- Legs of Iron (40)= *Greco Roman Empire (8:22)*
- Feet part Iron and part Clay (41)= *Confederacy of nations*
- Rock cut without hands (44,45)= *God of Heaven kingdom setup.*

Daniel Honored (vss. 46-49): As was promised by Nebuchadnezzar, Daniel is honored with "many gifts" and made "ruler over the whole province of Babylon and chief over all the wise men of Babylon" (48). Daniel makes a request to have his three friends to be rulers over the province of Babylon (49).

CHAPTER THREE

The events recorded in this chapter are self-explanatory. However, they also have a prophetic foreshadowing of events that will occur during the tribulation period.

The Image Erected (vss. 1-7): The image is most likely an image of Nebuchadnezzar himself (*just as the dream image was the image of a man, and he being the head*). Even though Nebuchadnezzar was only the head of gold in the dream, he covers the entire image in gold, showing his defiance and desire to rule over all the earth's empires (*4:28-30*). The image is 60 cubits high and 6 cubits wide (*90 feet high by 9 feet wide*), thus the number 6 is associated with it.

The command to worship the image that Nebuchadnezzar sets up is a foreshadowing of the time when all will be called to "worship the image of the Beast" (*Revelation 13:11-18*). *Notice this matter of forced worship does not have to be global.*

The Three Men Accused (vss. 8-12): The three Hebrews are refusing to disobey the commandment of God in Exodus 20:4, 5.

The Three Men's Refusal (vss. 13-18): Nebuchadnezzar reminds them of their punishment for refusal to obey his command, and states "*who is that God that shall deliver you out of my hands?*" The answer is the God of all the earth, in contrast to the gods of wood and stone (*Jer. 2:27,28*). Notice the response of Shadrach, Meshach and Abednego (17,18) is mixed with doubt, but they still stepped out by faith in God's ability to deliver.

The Fourth Man in the Fiery Furnace (19-25): The refusal of the Hebrews makes Nebuchadnezzar "*command to heat* *the furnace seven times more than it was wont to be heated"* (19). Shadrach, Meshach and Abednego were cast into the midst of the fire. Much to the astonishment of king Nebuchadnezzar he sees *"four men loose, walking in the midst of the fire and they have no hurt; and the fourth is like the Son of God"* (24,25).

The Three Men's Deliverance and Promotion (vss. 26-27): Shadrach, Meshach and Abednego are <u>not just delivered but</u>:

- Whose body the fire had no power over
- Nor was any hair on their head singed
- Neither was their coat changed
- Nor the smell of fire passed on them

The King makes the following decree and then promotes Shadrach, Meshach and Abednego: *"Therefore I make a decree, That every people, nation, and language, which speak any thing amiss against the God of Shadrach, Meshach, and Abednego, shall be cut in pieces, and their houses shall be made a dunghill: because there is no other God that can deliver after this sort."* (Daniel 3:29)

 The deliverance of Shadrach, Meshach and Abednego from the fiery furnace by the "Son of God" is a foreshadowing of the remnant within the remnant "saved" from the fiery judgment of the earth upon the Lord's return (Isaiah 1:9; Rev. 12:17; Zech.13:7-9; Matt. 3:11,12; Joel 1:15,19,20, 2:1,3; Mal. 4:1,2; 2 Pt. 3:7,10,11).

But now thus saith the LORD that created thee, O Jacob, and he that formed thee, O Israel, Fear not: for I have redeemed thee, I have called thee by thy name; thou art mine. When thou passest through the waters, I will be with thee; and through the rivers, they shall not overflow thee: when thou walkest through the fire, thou shalt not be burned; neither shall the flame kindle upon thee. (Isaiah 43:1-2)

In the coming Tribulation a Gentile ruler (Daniel 7:8) will demand for himself the worship that belongs to God (2 Thess. 2:4; Rev. 13:8). Any who refuse to acknowledge his right to receive worship will be killed (Rev. 13:15). Assuming political and religious power, he will oppress Israel (Rev. 13:7). Most of the people in the world, including many in Israel will submit to and worship him. But a small remnant in Israel, like the three friends in Daniel's day, will refuse. Many who will not worship the Antichrist will be severely punished; some will be martyred for their faithfulness to Jesus Christ. But a few will be delivered from those persecutions by the Lord Jesus Christ at His second coming.

CHAPTER FOUR

It is a remarkable thing that Nebuchadnezzar would give an autobiography of his pride, his temporary insanity, and his beastly behavior, and then give glory to the God of Israel for his recovery. (4:4-37)

Verses 1-3 were most likely written by Nebuchadnezzar following his recovery, and verses 28-33 by Daniel. Nebuchadnezzar had to learn the overall lesson, as is stated in the latter portion of verse 25:

"..till thou know that the most High ruleth in the kingdom of men, and giveth it to whomsoever he will." (Daniel 4:25)

The King's Dream (vss. 4-18): The king dreams a dream, and the thoughts upon his bed and the visions of his head troubled him (5). He made a decree *to bring all the wise men of Babylon to him to interpret the dream (6-7):

*Nebuchadnezzar's ability to cancel one of his laws and replace it with another is evidence of his might and personal power. Rulers of the Medo-Persian Empire, which replaced the Babylonian Empire, could not do this; it was impossible for them to override a previously written law- they had a type of constitutional monarchy (cf. 6:8, 12, 15).

The wise men were unable to tell Nebuchadnezzar the interpretation of the dream (18), so Daniel is brought in and Nebuchadnezzar tells to him the vision of the dream (8-18).

The Interpretation of the Dream (vss. 19-26): Daniel is troubled about the interpretation because it could mean his life; he knows the news is not toward the king

(27). Daniel reveals that Nebuchadnezzar's kingdom is the tree that has flourished and grown into a mighty kingdom (20-22). The cutting down of the tree symbolized the disgrace and removal of Nebuchadnezzar from the throne. The stump being left in the field with the dew from heaven on it whose dwelling is with the beasts of the field, is the judgment that Nebuchadnezzar will experience (23, 25). The stump being left was a promise that Nebuchadnezzar would one day reign again (26). Daniel ends this portion with the exhortation to turn from his prideful heart (27).

The Humbling of Nebuchadnezzar (vss. 28-33): God graciously gave king Nebuchadnezzar a full year to repent of his pride, but the king refused to yield and pride filled his heart (29, 30 cf. Ec. 8:11). Pride brought about Satan's fall (Isaiah 14) and Uzziah's downfall (2 Chr. 26:16-21). The Lord's voice interrupts the king's speech (31). The same hour was the king's heart turned into the heart of a beast (33).

The Restitution of Nebuchadnezzar (vss. 34-37): The first person narrative resumes in verse 34, for at the end of the seven years as God had promised, Nebuchadnezzar was delivered of his affliction and restored to a normal human life. It began with him "lifting up his eyes to heaven" (34, 35). Daniel ends by extolling the King of Heaven and the knowledge (personally) that "those that walk in pride he is able to abase."

The term "Most High" God is used repeatedly throughout this chapter and therefore is not without significance. The phrase "most High God" is in reference to God being the ruler of both aspects of His creation: heaven and earth. With this in mind, the term "knowledge" is used in reference to Satan and his fall, for he desired to be "like the most High God" ruler over heaven and earth (Isaiah 14). In our passage Nebuchadnezzar, in pride, saw himself (as Satan does) ruling over all the kingdoms of the earth. Thus, when his understanding returns to him he says, *"I blessed the most High, and I praised and honoured him that liveth for ever, whose dominion is an everlasting dominion, and his kingdom is from generation to generation"* (Daniel 4:34)

CHAPTER FIVE

In this chapter Babylonia's empire comes to an end; in a night the Medes and the Persians (arms and breast of silver) come and overtake the city without even a fight. God told Nebuchadnezzar that his kingdom would come to an end, and He accomplishes it in a most amazing way, a way in which He foretold 150 years before the event.

The scene in chapter five is that of a celebratory feast. This feast is going on at the very time that the Medo Persian empire is outside the city walls trying to invade this great city. The city of Babylon boasted that it was impregnable and that there was enough food stored away to feed the population for twenty years. With walls soaring 300 feet high and numerous towers, not to mention the Euphrates river flowing from the north to the south through in its midst, who was able to topple this great city?! With this false sense of security and pride, Belshazzar had a feast.

Belshazzar and His Great Feast (vss. 1-4): Outside the city walls of Babylon were the Medo Persian armies; inside were the Babylonians and in the very heart of the city Belshazzar King of Babylon held a feast. Belshazzar commands to bring in the vessels of gold and silver that Nebuchadnezzar had taken out of the temple of Jerusalem (II Chron. 36:10, 17-19; Jer. 52:17-23). They praised the gods that are no gods who speak not, nor see, nor can save! Keep this statement in mind as we look at Isaiah chapter 44 & 45 (See also Psalm 115;4-8).

The Writing On the Wall (vss. 5-16): The sight so troubled Belshazzar that he lost all control (6). The king, having not learned from his father in multiple areas, calls forth his wise men to read and interpret the dream, but they were unable to do so.

Why the Message was Sent (vss. 17-23): Daniel refuses the king's reward (17) and goes on to remind Belshazzar of the pride of his father and what God did to him, which Belshazzar knew (22). And now Belshazzar is following in his father's footsteps in bringing in the vessels of the Lord and using them to praise the gods of silver and gold, of brass and stone, glorifying not the God of his very breath (23).

The Interpretation and its Fulfillment (vss. 25-31): The interpretation is as follows:

- MeNe—God has numbered thy kingdom and finished it!

- Tekel—Not only thy kingdom is finished but "thou art found wanting." Belshazzar's days are numbered.

- PeRes—thy kingdom is divided (*a divided monarch of the Medes and Persians*)

In the night of this event Belshazzar the king of the Chaldeans was slain. In one night the chest and arms of silver now rule over Israel. Over 100 years before this very event, God set forth through the prophet Isaiah how Babylon would be overtaken:

- In Isaiah 44:1-20 God challenges all the gods that Israel was worshiping saying *"who, as I shall call?"* (7) In this statement God is challenging all the gods to "call it" to tell the future if they are able.

- In Isaiah 44:24-26 God declares it is He that is able to call it and in so doing He "maketh diviners mad, that turneth wisemen backward and maketh their knowledge foolish."

- Finally in Isaiah 44:27, 28 & 45:1, 2 He "calls it."

In 1879 a cylinder was discovered in Babylon that recorded in great detail the conquest of Babylon by Cyrus, king of Persia. Through these passages we see the veracity of the prophecy of Isaiah:

"Cyrus on his way to Babylon came to the banks of the Gyndes, a stream which, rising in the Matienian mountains, runs through the country of the Dardanians, and empties itself into the river Tigris. The Tigris, after receiving the Gyndes, flows on by the city of Opis[i.e., Baghdad], and discharges its waters into the Erythraean sea [i.e., the Persian Gulf]. When Cyrus reached this stream, which could only be passed in boats, one of the sacred white horses accompanying his march, full of spirit and high mettle, walked into the water, and tried to cross by himself; but the current seized him, swept him along with it, and drowned him in its depths. Cyrus, enraged at the insolence of the river, threatened so to break its strength that in future even women should cross it easily without wetting their knees. Accordingly he put off for a time his attack on Babylon, and, dividing his army into two parts, he marked out by ropes one hundred and eighty trenches on each side of the Gyndes, leading off from it in all directions, and setting his army to dig, some on one side of the river, some on the other, he accomplished his threat by the aid of so great a number of hands, but not without losing thereby the whole summer season.

Having, however, thus wreaked his vengeance on the Gyndes, by dispersing it through three hundred and sixty channels, Cyrus, with the first approach of the ensuing spring, marched forward against Babylon. The Babylonians, encamped without their walls, awaited his coming. A battle was fought at a short distance from the city, in which the Babylonians were defeated by the Persian king, whereupon they withdrew within their defenses. Here they shut themselves up, and made light of his siege, having laid in a store of provisions for many years in preparation against this attack; for when they saw Cyrus conquering nation after nation, they were convinced that he would never stop, and that their turn would come at last.

Cyrus was now reduced to great perplexity, as time went on and he made no progress against the place. In this distress either someone made the suggestion to him, or he bethought himself of a plan, which he proceeded to put in execution. He placed a portion of his army at the point where the river enters the city, and another body at the back of the place where it issues forth, with orders to march into the town by the bed of the stream, as soon as the water became shallow enough: he then himself drew off with the unwarlike portion of his host, and made for the place where [former queen] Nitocris dug the basin for the river, where he did exactly what she had done formerly: he turned the Euphrates by a canal into the basin, which was then a marsh, on which the river sank to such an extent that the natural bed of the stream became fordable. Hereupon the Persians who had been left for the purpose at Babylon by the, river-side, entered the stream, which had now sunk so as to reach about midway up a man's thigh, and thus got into the town. Had the Babylonians been apprised of what Cyrus was about, or had they noticed their danger, they would never have allowed the Persians to enter the city, but would have destroyed them utterly; for they would have made fast all the street gates which gave upon the river, and mounting upon the walls along both sides of the stream, would so have caught the enemy, as it were, in a trap. But, as it was, the Persians came upon them by surprise and so took the city. Owing to the vast size of the place, the inhabitants of the central parts (as the residents at Babylon declare) long after the outer portions of the town were taken, knew nothing of what had transpired, but as they were engaged in a festival, continued dancing and reveling until they learnt the capture but too certainly. Such, then, were the circumstances of the first taking of Babylon."

By this historical find we have the details of the events of the overtaking of Babylon and proving the trustworthiness of scripture:

- The Euphrates River is reduced in strength (Isaiah 44:27)
- Cyrus named by name over 100 years before his birth (Isaiah 44:28 cf. Ezra 1)
- God shall loose the loins of kings (Isaiah 45:1 cf. Daniel 5:5,6)
- The ease by which Cyrus took the city (Isaiah 45:1,2)

CHAPTER SIX

Daniel's Promotion in the Persian Government (vss. 1-3): When the Medo-Persian alliances overthrew the Babylonian Empire; it acquired much geographic territory that it proceeded to incorporate into its kingdom. The Persian Empire became the largest that the world had yet seen, eventually encompassing modern Turkey, Egypt, and parts of India and North Africa as well as Babylonia. Darius divided his realm into 120 provinces, and set a "protector of the realm" in charge of each one (cf. Esth. 1:1; 8:9). They reported to three commissioners, one of whom was Daniel. The God of Heaven would promote Daniel through Darius. Because of the vast geographical region that 120 satrapies entailed, this number and size of provinces would be consistent with the Persian Empire as historically ruled by Cyrus. As time passed, Daniel distinguished himself above the other leaders, even though he would have been in his 80s. These verses set the stage for what follows by helping the reader appreciate how Darius felt about Daniel.

The Conspiracy Against Daniel (vss. 4-9): The text does not say why the other officials wanted to get rid of Daniel. Perhaps his integrity made it difficult for them to get away with political corruption. Anti-Semitism appears to have been part of their reason (cf. v. 13; 3:12). The text stresses the outstanding personal integrity and professional competence of Daniel; God was with him. The accusers' plan was similar to that of the Babylonian officials who had tried to topple Shadrach, Meshach, and Abed-nego (Ch. 3). They knew that Daniel was a God-fearing man who did not worship pagan idols. So they set a trap for him believing that he would remain faithful to his faith. When Daniel had to choose between obeying his God or his government, his God came first (cf. v. 10). The leadership of the realm agreed to *"establish a royal statute, and to make a firm decree, that whosoever shall ask a petition of any God or man for thirty days, save of thee, O king, he shall be cast into the den of lions."* Under Persian law, the king was bound by the authority of a royal edict (vv. 8, 12, 15; cf. Esth. 1:19; 8:8). This was a constitutional monarch and made his power less than it would be under a monarchy alone such as under Nebuchadnezzar (cf. 2:39).

Daniel's Faithfulness and Darius' Predicament (vss. 10-15): The new decree did not deter Daniel from continuing to pray for the Jews' return from exile, "When Daniel knew that the writing was signed", he did as was his habit, "as he did a foretime" (Dan. 6:10). Daniel praying for the Jews to return to the land seems clear since Daniel possessed a copy of Jeremiah's prophecy (9:2; cf. Jer. 29:1, 7, 10). Jeremiah had written that God had promised to hear such prayers, if they were sincere and wholehearted, to restore the fortunes of the Jews, and to re-gather them to the Promised Land (Jer. 29:12-14). The events of Daniel 6 most likely have happened just before Cyrus issued his decree allowing the Jews to return from exile (2 Chron. 36:22-23; Ezra 1:1-4). Jews were to pray to the Lord facing Jerusalem (2 Chron. 6:21, 34-39). Daniel's colleagues expected that the edict would not deter Daniel from his regular prayers, even though it might cost him his life! After reminding Darius of his decree, the hostile officials informed the king that his prime minister elect had violated it and was therefore worthy of death. Notice that they described Daniel as "one of the exiles from Judah" (cf. 2:25; 5:13), showing their animosity towards Daniel. Daniel had so won the king's favor that Darius immediately began trying to rescue his friend. Darius became angry with himself for signing the decree (cf. 2:1; 3:13; 5:6, 9). This shows how much he respected and valued Daniel.

Daniel in the Lions' Den (vss. 16-18): Darius' parting words to Daniel are significant. One could render them, *"Thy God whom thou servest continually, he will deliver thee."* The idea is that Darius had tried to save Daniel and had failed. The den of lions was most likely a large pit in the ground with an opening above. Daniel had to be lifted up out of it (v. 23), and others when thrown into it fell down toward its bottom (v. 24). The king and his nobles sealed the stone that covered the opening to make sure no one would release Daniel. In contrast to Nebuchadnezzar, who showed no compassion for Daniel's three friends, Darius *"passed the night fasting"*.

Daniel's Deliverance and his Enemies' Destruction (vss. 19-24): Notice the care that Darius had for Daniel for he cried with a *"lamentable voice"*. Notice once again the care that Darius had for Daniel: "Then was the king exceeding glad for him. Thus, *"Daniel ... believed in his God"* (cf. Hebrews 11:33). The men that accused Daniel (and their children and wives cf. Numbers 16:27) were now brought and cast into the den of lions and were consumed before they reached the bottom, adding to the miracle of Daniel's deliverance.

Darius' Decree and Praise of the God of Daniel (vss. 25-28): This story ends, as previous ones in the book did, with the king praising and promoting the God of Daniel. It is as though God was giving two witnesses to His people Israel: Nebuchadnezzar and Darius. Both monarchs testified to the living and eternal God's unshakable sovereignty, grace, and power in heaven and on earth (cf. 4:3, 34-35). These testimonies certainly would have encouraged the Israelites to trust Him in spite of the circumstances of the exile.

CHAPTER SEVEN

There are 5 revelations in Daniel:

- *1st Revelation - Chapter 2*
- *2nd Revelation - Chapter 7*
- *3rd Revelation - Chapter 8*
- *4th Revelation - Chapter 9*
- *5th Revelation – Chapters 9-12*

All 5 of the revelations in Daniel build upon the preceding ones, adding further details, especially in regard to the final kingdoms, the ten nations confederacy under the Antichrist and our Lord's final kingdom. Example: The details behind the 10 toes starts out with little information in the first revelation, but by the last you have a host of information (*2:41, 42 cf. 7:7, 9 cf. 8:9-12 cf. All of chapter 11*). All commentators have problems when they try to remove the 2nd revelation given in chapter seven from the preceding revelation given in chapter 2 (*Anglo Israelism or British Israelism is an example of this problem*). Even though the beastly kingdoms are shown to be four (see the interpretation 7:17) it is right to acknowledge there being 5 kingdoms prior to our Lord's final kingdom. The reason for not mentioning the 5th kingdom is because the 5th kingdom comes out of the 4th (see Daniel 7:23-24). The standing kingdom is taken over by the next kingdom. This is why it does not have a beast associated with it, but it is right to call it a kingdom.

The reason why the world kingdoms are likened to beasts instead of metals, as they are in the first revelation, is because from here out these Gentile world kingdoms are going to be looked at on how they treat Israel (See 7:7–21 cf. Ps. 83). This is why Satan is Leviathan in Isaiah 27:1; it is Satan that swims among the nations controlling them (Rev. 12).

Four Great Beasts from the Sea (vss. 1-3): Four Great Beasts are "kings that shall arise out of the earth" (vs. 17). They arise out of the "great sea" being the Mediterranean sea (Numbers 34:6,7; Josh. 1:4, 9:1, 15:12; Ezek. 48:28). This is done to emphasize that all these kingdoms will be ones that will arise around that geographic location. The "great sea" also is a depiction of multitudes of people and nations, vs. 17. (See also: Isaiah 17:12, 13; Rev. 17:1, 15). The four winds of heaven represent God's judgment in moving people and nations to do His bidding (See Rev. 7:1-3; Zech. 6:1-6).

The First Great Beast (vs. 4): This first great beast is like a lion with eagle's wings which represents Nebuchadnezzar, whose kingdom started out as a devouring lion but then had a change of heart and treated Israel favorably in his latter reign. It is also descriptive of Nebuchadnezzar himself, who when lifted up in pride was turned into a beast (4:29-33). However, after an appointed time Nebuchadnezzar has a man's heart restored unto him (4:34-36) and extols the King of Heaven (4:37).

The Second Beast (vs. 5): This second beast is likened to a bear, which was raised up on one side, having three ribs in its mouth and was told to arise and devour much flesh (vs. 5). This second beast is the Medo-Persian empire that will arise out of the earth (*represented also by the ram and identified in Daniel 8:20*). The bear rising up on one side is the Medes coming to power first, even though the Persians will rise to greater power, as is represented by the ram's horn that grew higher than the other horn (8:3, 15). The three ribs represent the three nations taken in the western expansion under Cyrus (Isaiah 45:14): Egypt, Ethiopia and the Sabeans. After heading westward first, Cyrus then heads to the east, expanding the borders of his kingdom all the way to India; which is represented in the expression "arise and devour much flesh." *The three ribs could also be the three outer borders that the Persian empire expanded to: Egypt, India and Lydia. (Ezek. 30:5).*

The Third Beast (vs. 6): The third beast is like a Leopard which has upon its back four wings of a foul and having four heads. This third beast is the Grecian Empire that will arise "after" the Medo-Persian Empire (*represented also by the he-goat and identified in Daniel 8:21, 22*). The four wings represent the swiftness by which Alexander conquered. The four heads represent the four-fold division that the Grecian Empire would be divided into following his death (8:21); his kingdom being divided among his four generals. This four-fold division of the empire is known as the Tetrarch concept and would be maintained under Roman rule (Luke 3:19).

The Fourth Beast (vs. 7): The fourth beast is not given a likeness, just that it is "dreadful and terrible and strong exceedingly." The description of the "great iron teeth" makes the connection to the 4th kingdom of the 2nd revelation, the legs of iron; the Greco-Roman Empire (It needs to be looked at like this: it is a Greco-Roman Empire (See Rom. 1:16; 10:12; Gal. 3:28).

The Fifth Beastly Kingdom (vss. 7, 8): This fifth kingdom is represented by ten horns that come out of the fourth kingdom. (*We now receive additional information regarding this kingdom and will continue to do so as the revelations advance through Daniel.*) The ten horns are ten kings that shall arise "out of" the fourth kingdom (cf. vs. 24). A little horn will arise among them (8). This little horn is the man of sin that will have influence over the ten to the point where three of the kings are plucked up by the roots (8 cf. 24). He will be "diverse" from the other kings (24), as we will learn he will be a man of fierce countenance (8:23). He will have eyes as a man and a mouth speaking great things. The "great things" are words against the "most High" (25). He shall wear out the saints of the most High, thinking to change times and laws (25). The man of sin, through his influence with the ten nation confederacy, will seek to wear out the saints (Matthew 24:15-24) to the point that the name of Israel be no more in remembrance (Ps. 83). The wearing out issue will be advanced upon more as we progress through Daniel. It would consist of such things as invading the land and making war with the saints (20,21); dividing up the land for gain and changing Israel's times and laws (Dan. 11:31-39).

The Establishment of the Kingdom on the Earth (vss. 9-14): In the first revelation we are only told some basic facts concerning this final Kingdom:

And in the days of these kings shall the God of heaven set up a kingdom, which shall never be destroyed: and the kingdom shall not be left to other people, but it shall break in pieces and consume all these kingdoms, and it shall stand for ever. (Daniel 2:44)

However, now in this second revelation we are given additional details concerning the "God of Heaven" being established on the earth. The thrones were cast down (9): The thrones are the 10 horn (10 toes) kingdom mentioned previously. It is in the days of these kings that the God of heaven will set up His Kingdom, a Kingdom that will break in pieces and consume all others (2:44).

The Ancient of Days is none other than God the Father, as is seen by the fact that the Son of man is Jesus Christ in verse 13 (Matt. 26:64). His throne was like the fiery flame and His wheels as burning fire (9): This throne is the throne of God (Revelation 4, Ezekiel 10, 28). Thousand thousands ministered unto Him (10): These are none other than the angelic host that will come with God the Father to earth (Rev. 5:11).

The Judgment Was Set and the Books Were Opened (10): This judgment is the judgment of the nations that the Lord Himself will perform as one of His first initial acts as monarch of the earth (Matt. 25:31, 32). Jesus Christ comes to God the Father and receives from Him the Kingdom (14), in which He will fulfill Israel's role; Israel will be the Saints of the Most High God and will have dominion over the nations (22, 27; Rev. 5:9, 10).

Overview of the Establishment of the Kingdom: The above verses offer us an amazing picture of the establishment of the Kingdom of Heaven upon the earth. While we may not have a complete picture of all events surrounding this time we can marvel in the additional details given to us.

There are several occasions that Jesus Christ presents Himself to God the Father. Upon providing redemption for mankind, Jesus presents Himself to God the Father following His resurrection, prior to His ascension (John 20:17, 27). Then He ascends to the Father and seats Himself at His right hand until His enemies be made His footstool (Matt. 22:44; Hebrews 10:12,13). Once His enemies are made His footstool, He once again presents Himself to God the Father to receive the right to rule over the earth, at which time He will begin to have "His

Day" on the earth (Revelation 4,5). Then once He has cast down the thrones of authority on the earth, God the Father will come to earth and give the Kingdom to the Son of Man, Jesus Christ (Daniel 7:13,14; Luke 1:32,33).

CHAPTER EIGHT

Chapter eight once again builds upon the preceding revelation, only this time the head of gold, Babylon, is no longer in view, for they are passed from the scene.

The Vision at the River Ulai in the Palace at Sushan (vss. 1-2): Daniel receives the vision from the area of Sushan or Susa in some maps. He receives this revelation two years following the one in chapter seven (7:1 cf. 8:1).

The Vision of the Ram (vss. 3-4): The ram with the two horns is the Medo-Persia Empire as is given by the interpretation in verse 20. The one horn that rises up higher than the other is the kingdom of Persia that becomes larger and more powerful than the Medes (*like the bear vision that rises up on one side 7:5*). Daniel is in the eastern portion of the province of Babylon and sees the ram push westward, northward and southward, showing the great expansion that took place in relation to its predecessor Babylon (*Like the bear vision that was told to devour much flesh 7:5*).

The Vision of the He-Goat (vss. 5-8): The He-goat is the Grecian empire that would overtake the Medo-Persia Empire, as is given in the interpretation in verse 21. The ram came from the west and touched not the ground (5) which shows the great speed in which the Grecian empire took over (*like the leopard that had wings of a fowl 7:6*). The notable horn (5) is the first king of this empire, Alexander the Great (21). The four notable horns that come up following the death of the first (*Alexander the Great*) is the four-fold breakdown of the fourth kingdom, the Greco-Roman empire (22,23). This fourfold empire is seen in the leopard vision having four heads (7:6).

Little Horn (vs. 9): The little horn is identical to the little horn mentioned in the preceding revelation (7:8) and is said to be the *"king of fierce countenance"* in the interpretation that follows (23). The little horn <u>arises out of</u> one of the four notable horns or kingdoms. To understand which of the four kingdoms the little horn arises out of we must look at the directions that are mentioned in verse 9. The little horn waxed exceedingly strong towards the "south, and the east and toward the pleasant land" (9). Notice that the missing direction is the north, showing that this little horn is from the northern quadrant of the Greco-Roman empire and moves toward the remaining directions. (*Thus, we learn in the proceeding revelations of the "king of the North" or Syria, making him an Assyrian- Isaiah 14:12*).

Additional Revelation Regarding the Little Horn (vss. 10-14; 23-25): We are now going to receive additional information regarding this little horn that is to be added to the information given in the preceding chapters (7:8,20-21, 24-25).

Cast Down (vss. 10-12): The term "cast down" repeated throughout these verses shows the little horn's great influence as that "king of fierce countenance" and that all these verses are in reference to him waxing exceedingly great against the pleasant land!

- o Cast down some of the host of heaven and the stars to the ground and stamped upon them. (10)
- o Cast down the place of the sanctuary (11)
- o Cast down truth to the ground (12)

Magnified Himself (vs. 11): This little horn magnifies himself against the prince of the host, the Lord of Heaven, as is seen also by the interpretation in verse 24-25. (*We will learn more of this in the last revelation 11:36-38*). Paul also gives us information regarding this magnifying issue in 2 Thess. 2:3,4.

Against the Sanctuary and Sacrifices (vss. 11-12): The little horn will be successful in removing the daily sacrifices *(Jewish worship)* and the destruction of the sanctuary. This event was used of our Lord as a marker for the believing Remnant to flee into the mountains (Matt. 24:15). We will gain great details on this in the following revelations (9:27, 11:30-32).

Casting Truth Down (vs. 12): The little horn will practice and prosper. The practice that prospers is the little horn's craft (23, 24), which again is elaborated upon in the following revelations (11:38).

The Interpretation of the Vision (vss. 15-25): Daniel seeks for the interpretation of the meaning, which Gabriel gives in the following seven verses. We have commented on the interpretations throughout the preceding verses.

The Vision is True (vss. 26, 27): Antiochus Epiphanes ruled the Seleucid Empire from 175 BC until his death in 164. In most commentaries it is stated that it is Antiochus Epiphanes that is referred to as the little horn in Daniel chapter eight. What follows is why I believe this view is the wrong interpretation:

- The title "little horn" is mentioned in the previous revelation Daniel 7:8, 20-25 which could not possibly be Antiochus Epiphanes, because this little horn *comes out of* the 10 horns which are the final kingdoms before the Lord's Kingdom is established.

- The time schedule dictates that you place the "daily sacrifice" being taken away in the final 3 1/2 years of the Tribulation (Daniel 9:27).

- Our Lord places the events regarding the abomination that maketh desolate as a yet future event (Matt. 24:15).

The biblical evidence of what the little horn does cannot possibly fit Antiochus Epiphanes (8:10).

PROFILE OF THE LITTLIE HORN:

- Out of the 10 horns, which are 10 kings shall arise the little horn (Daniel 7:8, 24).
- He shall speak great words against the most High (Daniel 7:25).
- He shall wear out the Saints of the most High (Daniel 7:25).
- He shall think to change times and laws for 3 1/2 years (Daniel 7:25).
- He shall wax exceedingly great towards the south, east and toward the pleasant land (Daniel 8:9).
- Cast down some of the host and of the stars to the ground, and stamped on them (Daniel 8:10).
- He shall magnify himself over the prince of the people (Daniel 8:11).
- Daily sacrifices shall be taken away (Daniel 8:11).
- A host is given him against the daily sacrifice (Daniel 8:12).
- Truth shall be cast to the ground (Daniel 8:12).
- The Little Horn now titled the king of fierce countenance (Daniel 8:23).
- He shall seek to destroy the mighty and holy

people (Daniel 8:24).

- He shall cause craft to prosper (Daniel 8:24).

- He shall magnify himself (Daniel 8:25).

- By peace he shall destroy many (Daniel 8:25).

- He shall stand against the Prince of princes (Daniel 8:25).

CHAPTER NINE

What's the big deal: All Bible prophecy teachers, cults and heretics clamor over Daniel 9:24-27. The books that deal with these verses abound and interpretations vary from the complex to downright bazaar.

So what is the big deal about these verses? To appreciate the significance of these verses one needs to do what so many commentators fail to do, appreciate the verses (even chapters and books) previous.

The Time (vs. 1): The time in which this chapter is unfolding is in the "first year" of the Medes Empire. This is significant, for the first Gentile power is now coming to a close. Don't forget Daniel has the previous revelations of the 5 Gentile world powers clearly in his understanding. Babylon / Medo-Persian / Greece / Greco-Roman Empire / Beastly Empire of the Little Horn.

Daniel's Understanding (vs. 2): Daniel understands by the reading of the prophet Jeremiah that 70 years are determined upon Israel for the first captivity (Jeremiah 25:11,12 cf. Zech.1:12). And thereby understands that the time is at its completion. However Daniel does not know how long the next four Gentile powers that are to come are going to rule, he does not have the time element of the visions.

Daniel's Request (vs. 3): It is the time aspect that Daniel seeks to know. Thus, Daniel *"seeks by prayer and supplications, with fasting and sackcloth and ashes."* To understand the time that these succeeding Gentile nations are to rule over Israel is the purpose of Daniel's prayer and is the reason why it is a big deal when the answer comes in verses 24-27.

The Prayer (vss. 4-20): The prayer is long but notice two things, first that it is not all the prayer, but rather only a portion of the prayer, for Daniel is interrupted (21) before he completes his "speaking in prayer". Second, that the prayer is a repentant prayer that Daniel is placing himself in the position as a repentant Israelite in light of Leviticus 23.

Gabriel Interrupts the Prayer (vss. 21-23): Gabriel is the one sent to him upon the moment he started praying. His purpose is to give Daniel that for which he sought: *O Daniel, I am now come forth to give thee skill and understanding. (Daniel 9:22)*

The Answer (vss. 24-27): Now therefore we understand what the big deal is all about, these four verses contain the time for the final Gentile kingdoms' dominance over Israel and in turn mark the time in which the God of Heaven will establish His kingdom on earth. The full scope of the time is given in verse 24; 70 weeks to: *finish the transgression, and to make an end of sins, and to make reconciliation for iniquity, and to bring in everlasting righteousness, and to seal up the vision and prophecy, and to anoint the most Holy. (Daniel 9:24)* The transgression, sins and iniquities that need finish and make an end are those the nation has merited according to Leviticus 23. The 70 weeks is literally 70 7s or 70x7, totaling 490 years.

Verse 25 gives you the beginning and the end of the dates mentioned. Thus from the commandment to restore and build Jerusalem unto the Messiah is 7 weeks (or 7x7 = 49 years) and 62 weeks (or 62 x 7= 434), for a total of 483 years until the Messiah. That is very telling, for now Israel has a timeframe by which to operate to look for the Messiah. Notice however that it is a short 7 years to complete the end of 490 years and accomplish what was mentioned in verse 24.

DANIEL'S 70 WEEKS

Seventy weeks are determined upon thy people and upon thy holy city, to finish the transgression, and to make an end of sins, and to make reconciliation for iniquity, and to bring in everlasting righteousness, and to seal up the vision and prophecy, and to anoint the most Holy. -DANIEL 9:24

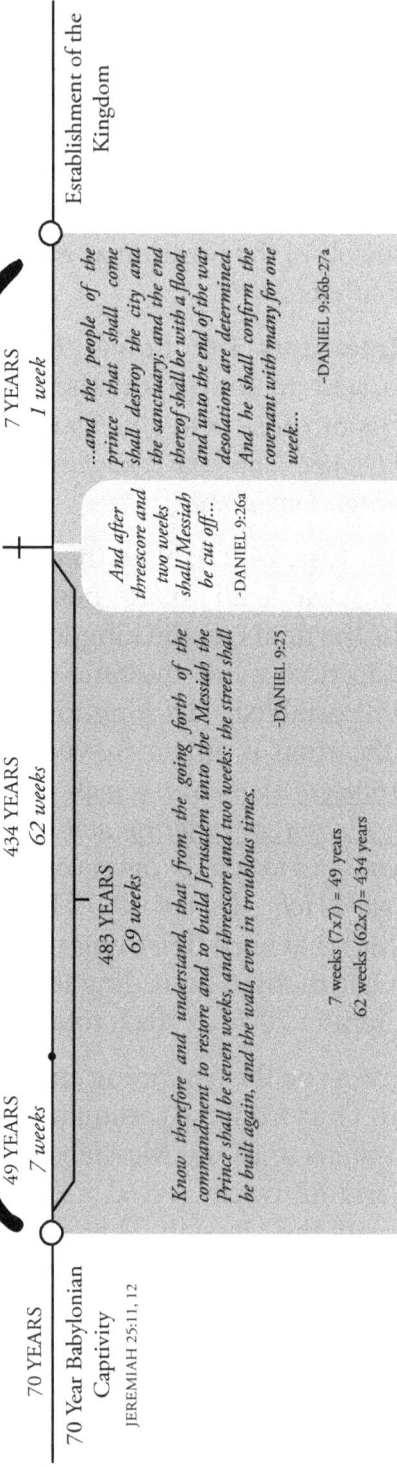

70 YEARS

70 Year Babylonian Captivity
JEREMIAH 25:11, 12

49 YEARS
7 weeks

434 YEARS
62 weeks

7 YEARS
1 week

Establishment of the Kingdom

483 YEARS
69 weeks

Know therefore and understand, that from the going forth of the commandment to restore and to build Jerusalem unto the Messiah the Prince shall be seven weeks, and threescore and two weeks: the street shall be built again, and the wall, even in troublous times.

-DANIEL 9:25

7 weeks (7x7) = 49 years
62 weeks (62x7)= 434 years

And after threescore and two weeks shall Messiah be cut off...
-DANIEL 9:26a

...and the people of the prince that shall come shall destroy the city and the sanctuary; and the end thereof shall be with a flood, and unto the end of the war desolations are determined. And he shall confirm the covenant with many for one week...

-DANIEL 9:26b-27a

Verse 26 now gives you information as to what happens at the end of the 483 years (the end of the 7 weeks and the 62 weeks), the Messiah will be cut off. This verse also gives you some details concerning the final week not accounted for in the previous verse. The latter half of this verse is not Titus the Roman but it is the "little horn" of Daniel chapter 7 and 8, which all the details concerning the people of the prince and the destruction of the city and the sanctuary have previously been addressed (*see. Luke 21:20-24, 7:7, 21; 8:9-13, 23-25*).

Verse 27 now goes over the final 7 years again only giving you the time and new added information concerning the covenant and other aspects transpiring at the middle of that week unto the end.

Thus, Daniel receives what he sought for by prayer, the time for the remaining Gentile kingdoms looking for the establishment of the Lord's Kingdom, heaven on earth.

CHAPTER TEN

This is the fifth and final revelation that is given to Daniel. (*1st: Daniel's image chapter 2 / 2nd: The beasts in Daniel 7 / 3rd : The Ram and He-goat chapter 8 / 4th : The Time Schedule chapter 9 / 5th : Time of the end or "latter days" chapter 11:2-12:4, 10-13.*) This final revelation will focus upon the last week of the time schedule. This is natural for it is the final week or 7 years that has the most events happening, as well as the greatest persecution against Israel (see vs. 14).

Daniel Seeks More Understanding (vss. 1-3, 12): Daniel is seeking understanding regarding the "latter days" (2, 3, 12, 14). This is the latter days of the total time given in the previous revelation, the last 7 years of the 490 years. He seeks additional information by fasting (2, 3, 12 *"chasten"*).

Daniel Sees the Lord of Glory (vss. 4-9): Daniel sees a *"certain man"* who is none other than the Lord of Glory (Rev. 1:12-17). This vision affects Daniel greatly: no Strength (8,16,17,); Deep sleep (9); Stood Trembling (11); Fear (12); Became as dumb (15); Sorrowful (16); No breath (17). Compare this reaction of Daniel with the reaction of John (1:17).

Gabriel is Sent to Make Known the Vision (vss. 10-14): In verse ten you have Gabriel being sent to make the vision known, just as he had in the past (8:16-19, 9:21-23). Gabriel comes at the beginning of Daniel's fast (2, 3 cf. 12, 13). Gabriel also is seen announcing the birth of John the Baptist and Jesus Christ (Luke 1:19, 26, 27). Gabriel appears to be the messenger for God.

The Battle in the Heavenly Places (vss. 13, 14, 20, and 21): It is of note that there is a battle transpiring in the heavenly places in connection to the ruling kingdoms on the earth. The battle in the spiritual realm is an amazing study of which these portions of Daniel lend to further information. Just as Gabriel appears to be the messenger of God Michael is the Archangel of God contending for the Nation of Israel (*see: Dan. 12:7, Jude 9, I Thess. 4:16, Rev. 12:7*).

CHAPTER ELEVEN

A Synopsis of the First Four Kingdoms (1-4): Babylon is passed from the scene so it is not in view, however picking up from there Gabriel gives a synopsis of the remaining empires:

- Medo-Persian Empire (1-2)

- Grecian Empire (2-3) - The mighty king is Alexander and when his kingdom is broken it is divided into the four-fold Greco-Roman Empire.

- Greco-Roman Empire (4) This kingdom will be "plucked up" even for others beside those. The idea is that this kingdom will be broken up even more, which it does under the 10 nation confederacy, the final kingdom prior to the LORD'S.

Wars and Rumors of Wars (vss. 5-20): In Matthew our Lord talks about this very time (Matthew 24:4-8). This time could be prior to the signing of the covenant with Israel.

League of Nations with the Vile Prince (vss. 21-27): It is out of the actions of wars and rumors of wars comes the "little horn" or "vile person" out of the land of the North (21). Thus he is the Assyrian (Isaiah 10). He will come in "peaceably" and through "flatteries"; the surrounding nations will make a "league" with him (21-24). This marks the beginning of the 7 year covenant and the last 7 years of Daniel's time schedule (Dan. 9:27).

Breaking of the Holy Covenant (vss. 28-45): At this time the "vile person" moves against the "holy Covenant" (28-30). He will pollute the sanctuary and place the abomination that maketh desolate (31). This time is mentioned by our Lord in Matthew 21-28 and is the marker for the mid-point of the tribulation (Dan. 9:27). This vile king shall kill many that do know their God (Israel) but they shall be rewarded in glory with white robes for their martyrdom (See. 11:34, 35; Dan. 12:3; Rev. 6:9-11; Dan. 7:9-14).

CHAPTER TWELVE

Completion of the Fifth Revelation (vss. 1-4): These verses complete the revelation given (11:2-12:1-4). It is concerning the "time of the end" (11:40) and will bring Daniel all the way to the establishment of the Kingdom (8:17; 11:35; 11:40; 12:9). Michael plays a key role in the tribulation especially at the latter end when our Lord comes back. This is seen in Michael "standing up".

- Michael is the Prince of thy people (12:1)
- Michael is called the Archangel (Jude 9)
- Michael has angels which he commands (Rev. 12:7-9)
- Michael will be involved in the deliverance of the believing remnant (12:1)

Time of Trouble (vs. 1) - This is none other than the tribulation period and can also refer to just the latter 3 1/2 years (Matt. 24:21;

Deliverance for thy People (vs. 1) - The issue of the Remnant of Israel being delivered from the "tribulation" is taught throughout Israel's scriptures (*Zeph. 2:2-3; Luke 21:36; Joel 2:31,32; They are hid in Babylon for the latter 3 1/2 years Rev. 12:13-17; Mich. 4:10 and are removed before its destruction Rev. 18:4*).

The book is the book of remembrance found in Malachi 3:16.

A Resurrection (vs. 2) - Other believing Remnant will be martyred however, but will still be resurrected and placed in the Millennium (See. 11:34,35; Dan. 12:3; Rev. 6:9-11; Dan. 7:9-14).

They that be Wise (vs. 3) - See vs. 10 — These "wise ones" are they that "watch" and "pray" looking for the Lord's return and have conduct accordingly and if so they will be "accounted worthy to escape" the latter 1/2 of the tribulation (Matt. 25:1-13; Luke 21:36)

Shine as the Brightness (vs. 3) - Those wise ones as previously mentioned will "shine as the brightness" which is a reference to them getting their white robes and placed in the kingdom in the Millennium. (See. 11:34,35; Dan. 12:3; Rev. 6:9-11; Dan. 7:9-14)

Seal up the Book (vs. 4) - See vs. 9 also. Daniel is told to seal up the vision, thus there is not a thirteenth chapter to Daniel as is contained in the Apocrypha by the title "Bel and the Dragon".

Running to and Fro & Knowledge Shall Increase (vs. 4) — The revelation is sealed up until the time of the end at which time "many will run to and fro and knowledge shall be increased". The running to and fro is the issue of the 400 silent years as prophesied by Amos 8:11,12 that there would be no words coming from God (*which covers the bulk of the time schedule*). This time of silence would end however with the coming of John the Baptist prophesying in the Judean wilderness running through the early Acts period (Mal. 3:1, Isaiah 40:1-3); and it was during this time that "knowledge was increased via the Epistles of Hebrews through Revelation (*especially Revelation*).

Desiring More Information (vss. 5-9): Daniel is still on the banks of the river Hiddekel (cf. 10:4). He sees two other men (angelic host) standing on either side of the river. One of them asked the man "clothed in linen" which was upon the waters, "How long shall it be to the end of these wonders?" (7).

The Man Clothed in Linen (vss. 6-7) - This man is the same mentioned at the beginning of the revelation in chapter 10:5 and is therefore the Lord of Glory. He answers the question with the length of the latter half of the tribulation: a time, times and an half (See. 1,260 days Rev. 11:3; 12:6; Times, time and dividing of time Dan. 7:12; Rev. 12:14).

Daniel Understands Not (vss. 8-9): Daniel does not understand this answer so asks again the questions at which time he is told to "Go thy way Daniel" (see vs.4).

Two Additional Dates (vss. 10-13): The wise that understand that are made white and tried have been addressed under verse 3. Daniel is given two additional pieces of information concerning the time of two specific events.

The removal of the Daily Sacrifice and the Setting up of the Abomination that Makes Desolate (vs. 11) - Daniel is given the time that the daily sacrifice shall be taken away and the abomination that maketh desolate is set up. This time is 1,290 days. That time is 30 days longer than the half of the tribulation (Rev. 11:3), making the time between the Sacrifices taken away and the Abomination set up 30 days.

The Time Daniel Will Stand in His Lot at the End of the Days (vss. 12-13) - The last date given is the date for when those righteous individuals, Daniel included will stand in their lot, at the end of days, in the Millennial Kingdom. The time in which this resurrection takes place is 1,335 days from the middle of the tribulation, making it 75 days into the Millennium once the 1,260 days of the latter half of the tribulation are completed.

...Then said I, O my Lord, what shall be the end of these things?
DANIEL 12:8-13

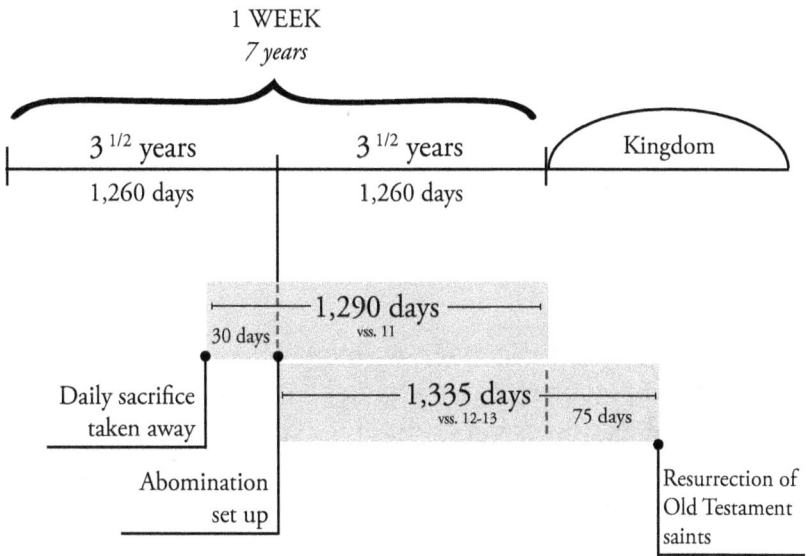

1 WEEK
7 years

3 ¹/² years

1,260 days

3 ¹/² years

1,260 days

Kingdom

30 days

1,290 days
vss. 11

Daily sacrifice
taken away

1,335 days
vss. 12-13

75 days

Abomination
set up

Resurrection of
Old Testament
saints

CONCLUSION

One cannot place too much importance in the book of Daniel. Because the LORD gave to Daniel the revelations in this book, we now have a timeline in which all prophetic events can be placed. As stated in this booklet, Daniel is placed in the middle of the prophets for a reason; it is the time line that all the events recorded in the Major and Minor Prophets are to be placed. So when it comes to God's dealings with the nation of Israel we have a time line of events.

It would be fitting here to mention one more major revelation given to us that has a bearing on this timeline, and that is the revelation given to the Apostle Paul concerning the Church the Body of Christ. It is through this revelation that we are to understand why it is that all the end events recorded by Daniel have not already come to pass. It is through the revelation given to Paul that we understand Israel's prophetic events are on hold while God forms His Body, the Church. Thus through the writings of Paul we have the completed Revelation of God.